WHAT HAPPENED NEXT?

GREAT
EXPLORERS

Richard Tames

WATTS BOOKS

LONDON • NEW YORK • SYDNEY

© 1995 Watts Books

Watts Books
96 Leonard Street
London
EC2A 4RH

Franklin Watts Australia
14 Mars Road
Lane Cove
NSW 2066

UK ISBN: 0 7496 1651 1

10 9 8 7 6 5 4 3 2 1

A CIP catalogue record for this book is available from the British Library.

Series editor: Belinda Weber
Designer: Cassedy Design Company; Edward Kinsey
Illustrator: David Penfound
Picture researcher: Diana Morris

Photographs: e.t. archive: 6l (Monument by Alonso de Mena in gilt and polychrome wood), 14b (Flying fish by de Bry), 15b, 13tc, 20l, 21r, 23t (Portrait of James Cook by Nathaniel Dance), 25l, 28r (Death of Cook by J. Clevely); Associated Press: 34t; Bridgeman Art Library: Cover, 4c, 5t (Anonymous portrait of Columbus), 7tl (Following the Stars – Livres des Merveille), 7tr, 9r (Chart of Juan Dela Cosa of Western Hemispere); 10t (Columbus in Chains by Lorenzo Delleari), 10c © National Maritime Museum (Map of World after 1492), 17t © Giraudon, 17b (Map of Mexico and South America), 18l © British Library (Chart by Bastian Lopez), 22l (Death of Moctezuma from Codex of Bernardo di Sahagun), 36r © Scott Polar Research Institute, 39t © Scott Polar Research Institute, 40t; Bruce Coleman: 11br © Alain Compost, 13tr © Rinie van Meurs; James Davis 26t; Mary Evans Picture Library: 22t, 29t, 30c, 31br,32t; Fotomas Index: 29b; Michael Holford: Cover 11l (Ptolemaic map of the world), 12l, 13b (The Vaz Durado map of the Magellan Straits), 17r, 18b, 24l, 26b, 28t, 31t, 31l, 32b, 34c (Death of Franklin by T. Smith); Mansell Collection: 6b,7b (Columbus on ship by de Bry), 12t, 25tr; Norsk Sjofartsmuseum: 37b, 38b; Popperfoto: 4br, 35c, 35br, 36l, 36b, 37t, 37c, 38b, 39b,40l; Royal Geographical Society: 33 tSouth American Pictures: 21b (Vera Cruz Diego Rivera), 22cr; Syndication International: 4t, 5c © Macdonald (World map c. 1489), 8b, 9b, 11tr, 16b © coll. Bibliotheque Nationale, 19tl © Galeria Cano, Bogota/Rudolf Schrimpff, 19c, 27c © BPCC/Aldus Archive, 33b © Trustees of the British Museum, 33c ©Peabody Museum Harvard University, 34b, 35t © Fram Museum/photo Millet; Wallace Collection: 14b, 20t; Zefa: 9t © James Watt, 15tr, 27t © Holdsworth, 27b © Erwin Christian.

Printed in Belgium.

CONTENTS

The oldest reason for exploration is to find somewhere better to live. Around AD 800 the Maori peoples began to leave Polynesia (probably Tahiti) in huge canoes and settle in New Zealand. In AD 986 a Norwegian, Erik the Red, led an expedition from Iceland to Greenland. Later Vikings went even further and settled in Newfoundland. Between 1804 and 1806 the Americans, Lewis and Clark, crossed the interior of the United States to the Pacific coast. Their reports encouraged people to move away from the eastern coast and settle in the west.

Seafaring explorers used astrolabes to monitor their position.

WHY EXPLORE?

THE FIRST TRAVELLERS

One of the first people to travel out of sheer curiosity was the Arab, Ibn Battuta. He set out from Morocco in 1325 on a pilgrimage to Mecca and went on travelling for the next 30 years. He visited India, China, Africa and Spain and covered about 75,000 miles, meeting over 60 kings and 2,000 other important people.

THE GREAT MOTIVATOR

Trade was a major reason for exploration in the 15th and 16th centuries. Portuguese kings sent expeditions along the coast of Africa, searching for a sea-route to India. Vasco da Gama finally found one in 1499. From then on Europeans could buy spices like pepper and cloves direct from India, rather

Pirates and unfriendly natives were common problems for explorers. So explorers and their crews carried swords or guns to defend themselves.

than from Arab merchants who brought them overland to the Mediterranean. This created a profitable new sea-borne trade between Europe and Asia involving silk, porcelain, cottons, jewels and tea as well as spices.

THE SPANISH

The Spanish conquistadors who explored and then conquered Central and South America in the 16th century went "For God and for Gold". They forced the local people to work as slaves in mines and on plantations but claimed that they had saved their souls by converting them to Christianity.

A SCIENTIFIC APPROACH

From the 17th century onwards explorers became more scientific in their approach. Captain Cook took artists and scientists with him on his voyages through the Pacific. In 1833-6 the scientist Charles Darwin sailed right round the world in *HMS Beagle*. By comparing plants and animals in different countries he was able to work out his theory of evolution, which explained how creatures had developed in different parts of the world.

MODERN EXPLORERS

In the 20th century exploration has become more of a carefully planned team-effort, often relying on advanced technology. But there have still been many examples of heroic exploration by individuals or small groups. In 1930 the British traveller Bertram Thomas became the first European to cross the 'Empty Quarter' of the Arabian desert. In 1947 Norwegian Thor Heyerdahl sailed a small raft, the *Kon-Tiki*, from South America to Polynesia to show that Polynesians might have migrated to their islands like that. And in 1993 the English explorer Sir Ranulph Fiennes became the first person to cross the Antarctic on foot.

Captain Robert Falcon Scott – a polar explorer.

Columbus Searches For The New World

1490

Christopher Columbus became a sailor at an early age, and was convinced that it was possible to reach the East by sailing West.

Cristoforo Colombo, a nobody from the Italian port of Genoa, claims that he can reach the East by sailing West! More and more leading experts do seem to agree - despite what common sense tells us - that the world is round and not flat. *(Though they can't yet explain why we don't fall off it!)*

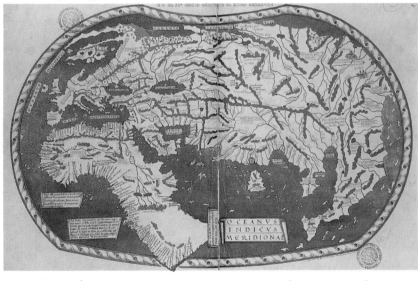

The known world in 1489, before Columbus' voyages. Many such maps relied on guesswork and the imagination of the map-maker rather than established fact.

So, in theory, it should be possible to reach the East by travelling West – but how far do you have to go before the West becomes the East? The man from Genoa has done some calculations about the distances involved and seems to believe that it's much nearer than anyone else thinks.

SAYS WHO?

Would you trust this man with your life? After all, who is he? Colombo's father was just a poor weaver – not even a seaman. He has had quite a lot of sailing experience – as far east as the Greek islands, as far south as Madeira and as far north as – where? Somewhere very cold – but nobody, not even Colombo himself, seems quite sure where. And he's been shipwrecked off the coast of Portugal which is where he's been living for some years with his brother, a map-maker.

Colombo's first name, Cristoforo – as every Christian knows – means 'Christ-bearer' and he certainly comes across as a man with a mission.

He even says he hears voices from God. And he says his ideas about sailing West to go East are based on the Bible.

WHO WILL PAY?

Of course, the Colombos of this world are always looking for someone else to put up the money for their schemes. In 1484 the King of Portugal turned him down flat. And why? Because his experts told him that Colombo was way off in his calculations and that existing ships could not sail these distances. And has anyone got better advisers than the King?

But Colombo is not a man to give up that easily. He has also tried the rulers of England, France and Spain for their backing. In 1490 a Spanish panel of experts advised King Ferdinand and Queen Isabella that the project – quote – "appears impossible to translate into reality to any person with any knowledge, however limited, of these questions." In plain language – it's not on, Colombo!

5

1492

Ferdinand II of Aragon and Isabella I of Spain finally agreed to fund Columbus' expedition in August 1492.

Columbus (also Colombo [Italian], Colom [Portuguese] and Colon (Spanish) - despite being turned down in 1490 - kept on at the King and Queen of Spain to support him. Perhaps they were finally won over because he was so confident of success that he demanded to be made governor of every land he discovered AND to have ten per cent of all the gold, jewels, spices and trade that resulted from his discoveries.

A ROYAL SEND OFF

The King and Queen came in person to see Columbus off at dawn on 3 August 1492. His fleet consisted of the *Santa Maria* of 100 tons and the *Nina* and *Pinta*, which were each about half that size. Of the 90 men and boys on board almost every one was a Spaniard.

The Santa Maria was originally built as a small trading ship. She was the flagship of the fleet, as well as the storeship. She carried the supplies of fresh water and food needed to keep all the crew alive on the voyage.

Main mast

Light swivel gun

Hold with stores and provisions

Bowsprit

The signature of Christopher Columbus.

.S.
.S. .S.
X M Y
Xpo FERENS

OFF TO GO TO THE
THE EARTH

All seafarers need to know their whereabouts at sea and many relied on astrolabes to keep track of their position.

INTO THE UNKNOWN

On 12 August the fleet reached the Canary Islands. Over three weeks then passed in loading supplies and making last-minute repairs. At dawn on 6 September the fleet set sail again. Three days later the men on board took their last look at the known world as it slipped below the horizon.

WHERE ARE WE GOING?

Progress was good until 18 September. But then the winds fell. The ships slowed to a crawl. The sailors began to curse and complain. None of them –

not even the oldest – had ever been out of sight of land for so long. As sailors they agreed with the experts – the world WAS round. But how BIG was it? The experts didn't agree about that. And the sailors certainly didn't know. What

An engraving of Columbus on the voyage to find the East.

if the food and water ran out before they reached land? One by one they would die on this endless, endless sea...

IS HE LYING TO US?

Every ship's captain keeps a log-book. Columbus kept two.

The log-book has a daily record of the ship's position, the state of the sea, the weather and the condition of the crew. Columbus knew that things were going badly wrong. The men were grumbling and fighting amongst themselves. The voyage seemed to be taking far longer than he had calculated. So he kept two log-books. One recorded the real distance his ships had covered. The other had false figures which he showed to the crew to convince them that they weren't as far from Spain as they thought.

CHANGING COURSE

A few days after the wind dropped the look-out thought he saw land. But he was mistaken. By 25 September the wind was so light and the sea so calm that the crew began to mutter about turning back before it was too late. If they left now, they could get home before they ran out of food and water.

On 2 October the wind suddenly picked up. Great flocks of birds were seen flying south-westwards. Columbus ordered a change of course to follow them. Another week passed. Still no sight of land. The muttering began again. *Will Columbus find land?...*

Making sure there was enough food for everyone to eat was another problem of long voyages. The ships carried bacon, salted fish, cheese and hard biscuits stored in barrels. But they had no way of keeping the food fresh and most of it rotted on the long voyage and weevils ate the biscuits.

What if the crew ran out of food before they reached land and could resupply their ships? True, they could catch fresh fish and the occasional seabird or dolphin but would this be enough to keep 90 men alive and for how long?

Fresh water was also a problem. What if they ran out before the reached land? Would they simply starve to death or die of thirst in the middle of an endless ocean?

WAS THERE A MUTINY?

Although they had grumbled, and even talked of turning back, the men knew that they were sailing on an expedition that had been paid for by the King and Queen. The crews were Spaniards, almost to a man, and Catholics every one. The church had blessed the voyage. The King and Queen had commanded it. A mutiny would be both an unlawful rebellion and a sin.

But did men owe it to God or their rulers to obey commands that would lead to certain death? Surely that would be as bad as deliberately committing suicide – a terrible sin in the eyes of the Catholic Church. And the commander was a foreigner. Should they really trust him like a Spaniard?

The problem with a mutiny was that there were three ships, and not just one. Suppose Columbus' own ship, *Santa Maria*, stayed loyal to him while the others mutinied. She was by far the biggest of the fleet. She could just sail on and abandon the other two ships – or even use her guns to blow them out of the water. If there was a successful mutiny, what would happen then? If Columbus was killed how could the mutineers explain this back in Spain? Wouldn't the King and Queen be suspicious if only Columbus was killed. Should they kill some of the other officers and crew to make it look more convincing, and if so, who? If they cooked up a story about Columbus falling sick – or even overboard – could they all trust each other to stick to it? Even under torture? And if they took Columbus back alive how would they make him keep quiet? – or could they convince the King and Queen that he really was mad?

The sailors of Columbus' crew carried swords with which to defend their ships from attack. They could also have been used for mutiny.

WHAT HAPPENED NEXT?

WAS COLUMBUS LOST?

Columbus had studied the science of ocean navigation on his earlier voyages, but did that make him an expert? He had also been shipwrecked off the coast of Portugal – what if this had been the result of poor navigation? All the sailors knew that navigators had to rely on simple instruments – a compass to show which direction the ship was heading, an astrolabe to measure the height of the Sun or stars and so show the ship's north-south latitude, and constantly turned hour-glasses

Navigation instruments were crude. Here a sailor is using an astrolabe.

The crew may have caught dolphins to supplement their meagre rations.

DID THE SUPPLIES RUN OUT?

Columbus and his crew had been sailing for 35 days without seeing land.

Had Columbus made a mistake in his calculations? Was the world really much bigger than he had imagined? How could he persuade his crew to keep going?

CAN YOU DECIDE THE REAL FATE OF COLUMBUS?

to time each stage of the ship's journey, letting the sailors work out the east-west longitude. Even with these special instruments, navigators were often forced to rely on 'dead reckoning', where they estimated the ship's position from their course, speed and likely drift downwind. What if Columbus had made a mistake in these calculations? Would the crew continue sailing forever, without finding land?

An astrolabe is a navigational instrument used to measure the height or altitude of the Sun in order to establish the north-south latitude.

C olumbus was a man with a mission. The men who signed on with him surely knew what they might be getting into. And they certainly knew the penalty for mutiny – particularly on a royal expedition. Columbus couldn't put down a mutiny single-handed. But if enough men – men the others respected – stood by him, then he certainly could.

Suppose Columbus put down a mutiny, what then? Suppose they sailed on with their food and water supplies getting ever lower and found nothing. Might not even Columbus have turned back? Or suppose he went on regardless – and failed to find land anywhere. He had already changed course once to follow a flock of birds. Suppose he saw another flock, or some drift-wood, and changed course again? Into the endless ocean...

Or finally, suppose he had actually succeeded in reaching China. What if the Chinese people mistook him and his crew for pirates and just locked them up or executed them? – Would the King and Queen of Spain send anyone rescue them?

Columbus' voyages discovered so much new land that maps had to be redrawn. This one shows the known western hemisphere in 1500.

DID COLUMBUS REACH CHINA?

WHAT REALLY HAPPENED TO CHRISTOPHER COLUMBUS?

O n 10 October a mutiny finally broke o u t . C o l u m b u s promised that if no land were sighted within three days he would turn back. The very next evening he – and the look-outs – saw a dim light ahead. But it disappeared. At 2 a.m. the following day grey coral reefs were seen. It was land – and no mistaking this time.

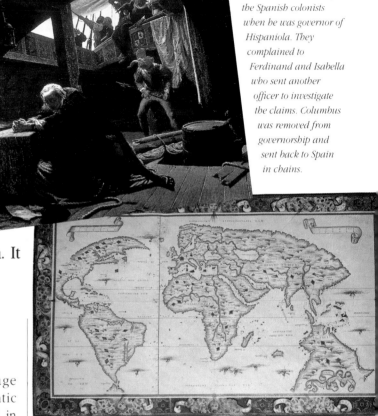

Columbus was hated by the Spanish colonists when he was governor of Hispaniola. They complained to Ferdinand and Isabella who sent another officer to investigate the claims. Columbus was removed from governorship and sent back to Spain in chains.

Following Columbus' voyages, map-makers had to rethink how the world looked and their new maps show a much more recognisable world.

THE NEW WORLD

Columbus finally landed on an island in the Bahamas. With the help of a local Arawak Indian acting as his pilot he explored nearby islands, hoping to prove that he had landed in Japan. In fact he found Cuba – which he thought was part of China – and then Haiti.

GOLDEN TREASURES

After a perilous voyage back across the Atlantic Columbus was received in triumph in Spain, bringing with him samples of gold, amber, parrots – and Indians. Six months later, in September 1493, he returned to 'the Indies' at the head of a fleet of 17 ships carrying 1,500 people

to colonise the newly claimed territories. On this voyage Columbus visited more Caribbean islands, including Jamaica, Guadeloupe and Puerto Rico. Unfortunately he also found more gold – which made the colonists forget about farming in favour of getting rich quickly by prospecting.

HOME IN CHAINS

Columbus came back twice more. On his third voyage he visited Trinidad and the coast of the South American mainland. But

when a rebellion broke out in the new Spanish Caribbean colonies while he was away exploring he was blamed and shipped back home in chains. Although the King and Queen freed him at once, they never really trusted him again. On his fourth and last voyage he sailed along the coast of Central America but when he got back to Spain he realised his career was at an end. He died on 20 May 1506, rich, but lonely and bitter – and still thinking that he had discovered a new route to the East, not a 'New World'.

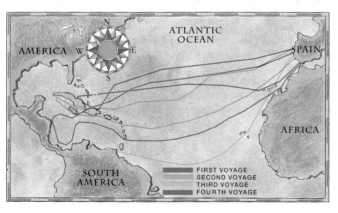

The map showing the route of Columbus' four voyages. He added dramatically to our knowledge of the world. His voyages discovered the major islands of the West Indies, South America, and much of Central America.

Magellan Believes That The World Is Round ⟨1512⟩

The spice-rich Molucca Islands really belong to Spain, not Portugal! This astonishing claim has been put forward by - a Portuguese! - who says he is now a Spaniard!

Ferdinand Magellan argued with the King of Portugal, then swore allegiance to the King of Spain.

The world was a mysterious place before it was accurately mapped. This map was drawn by Ptolemy

POPE CHALLENGED

Fernando de Magellanes has challenged the decision made in 1493 by His Holiness the Pope that all territories lying east of his north-south demarcation line should rightfully belong to Portugal, while those to the west should belong to Spain.

GOING WEST

As every spice-merchant knows the Moluccas are reached by sailing east round Africa and across the Indian Ocean.

Magellanes claims that he can reach them by

Spices, such as ginger, pepper, chillies and cloves, were valuable commodities fetching high prices in European countries.

sailing west – in the opposite direction.

If he succeeds this will prove that the world is indeed ROUND.

CAN HE BE TRUSTED?

Magallanes, as he calls himself, was born a Portuguese and was called Fernao de Magalhaes. As a young man he took part in the fighting which gave Portugal control of the Indian Ocean spice trade. No-one doubts his bravery. But his career came to a stop after he was crippled in the leg fighting in Morocco. Magallanes asked the King of Portugal for a raise in pay. The King refused. Magallanes asked again. The King refused again – and told him his services were no longer needed. So now he says he's a Spaniard.

MAGELLAN SAILS IN

Victoria was one of the five ships in which Magellan set out.

Magellan (to use the English form of his name) left Spain on 20 September 1519 with a fleet of five ships and 270 men from nine different countries. They crossed the Atlantic and then sailed down the coast of South America looking for a way through to the great ocean that lay beyond it. Magellan knew that the ocean was there because it had been seen by Balboa when he marched across Panama in 1513. But Magellan did not know for certain how to reach it.

Turning an hourglass regularly allowed sailors to keep track of their position.

MUTINY!

Supplies began to run low so Magellan put his men on short rations. The men were cold. They were worried. And now they were hungry.

At midnight on Easter Day 1520, a group of officers led a mutiny against him. One of them was certainly acting as a spy for the King of Portugal, who desperately wanted the voyage to fail.

Magellan still knew which of his men he could count on and acted quickly. One of the mutinous officers was hacked to pieces in a fight, another was tried and hanged, while a third was simply left to survive by himself on the shore of South America.

THE STRAIT

Magellan did finally find a passage which enabled him to lead his fleet round the tip of South America – but not before one ship had been wrecked and another had deserted.

It took 38 days battling against strong winds to

When the food supplies ran out, sailors were forced to eat whatever they could find – like rats, sawdust and old sailcloths.

O THE UNKNOWN!

Sailors often carried knives with which to defend themselves against pirate attacks.

Explorers must have expected to see many exotic animals on their travels. These penguins must have seemed strange when first seen.

pass through what is now called the *'Strait of Magellan'*. When, at last, they saw the open sea ahead of them, Magellan finally broke down and wept.

A PACIFIC DISASTER

At first Magellan and his men had such a smooth voyage across the 'Sea of the South' that they decided to re-name it 'Pacific' meaning peaceful.

But they had no idea just how big the ocean was. Magellan thought it would take a month to reach the Moluccas. In fact it would take four times as long.

Day after day they drifted on. Their water supplies ran so low that they were tortured by thirst. As the food ran out, they ate rats and soup made from sawdust and the leather coverings off their ships' rigging. It was 99 days before they finally landed on the island of Guam and found fresh food. By this time, 19 men had died.

A PACIFIC TRUIMPH

From Guam, Magellan sailed towards the islands now known as the Philippines and landed on the island of Cebu. The ruler was very impressed by Magellan's strange ships and by the guns and swords carried by his men. He quickly agreed to convert to Christianity and become an ally of the King of Spain.

But the people of the neighbouring island of Mactan immediately rebelled against him for doing this. So the King of Cebu turned to Magellan for help. He asked Magellan to help him put down the rebellion... ***Will Magellan help the King of Cebu fight the Mactans?...***

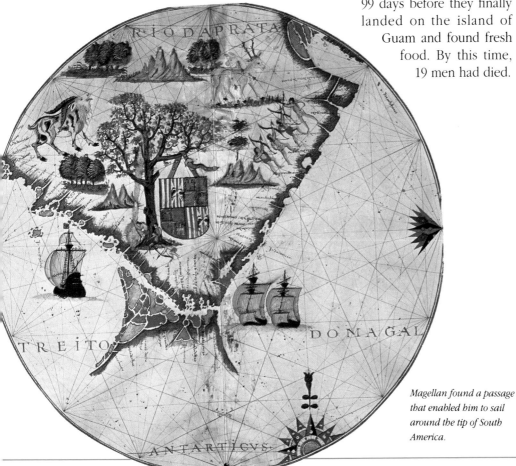

Magellan found a passage that enabled him to sail around the tip of South America.

DID MAGELLAN ATTACK MACTAN?

Magellan and his men had been travelling for 18 months. He had already lost two of his ships. His remaining men had only just begun to recover from three months of near-starvation. Would they be fit for a fight? And even if they were, should he risk them?

On the other hand, if he refused to fight would the King of Cebu think he was a coward, or a traitor – and turn against him? Although they had far superior weapons, Magellan and his men would be easily outnumbered and could be overpowered.

But suppose it was a trap? Why had the ruler of Cebu agreed so quickly to become a Christian and the ally of the King of Spain? Did he just want to take advantage of Magellan's ships and men to conquer Mactan – which might not really have been his at all. Would he remain loyal to Spain even after Magellan had left? Or was he secretly an ally of the people of Mactan, plotting to lure the strangers into a trap and kill them so they could take their ships and weapons?

Should Magellan trust him with his own life and those of his crew? And why should he jeopardise the whole purpose of his expedition – getting to the Moluccas – just to attack some island about which he really knew nothing?

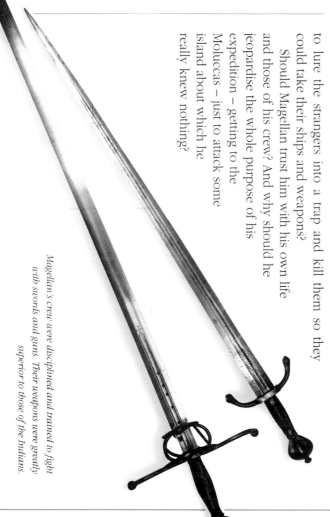

Magellan's crew were disciplined and trained to fight with swords and guns. Their weapons were greatly superior to those of the Indians.

Everyone on board the ship had a specific job to do. Without a full crew, would Magellan be able to sail anywhere?

WHAT HAPPENED NEXT?

DID MAGELLAN WIN?

Even if they were outnumbered Magellan's men would have been much better armed than anyone they might have to fight. The people of Mactan might have had spears and slings, blow-pipes and even bows and arrows. But Magellan's men had swords, guns, cannons and crossbows, and wore steel armour to protect themselves. And they were experienced and disciplined soldiers. Would the people of Mactan offer much resistance to such a force? And even if they tried, Magellan's superior firepower would surely ensure success.

On long sea voyages, food preservation was always a problem. Foods, such as beans and garlic, were chosen as they could be stored in casks. Fresh foods were rare and a luxury at sea.

DID MAGELLAN LOSE?

Magellan's men might have been much better armed than the people of Mactan – but they were fighting on unknown territory. The people of Mactan were fighting on home ground. They could easily lay traps or simply pick off Magellan's men in ones and twos as they wandered around looking for a place to attack.

What if Magellan and his men were overpowered? They might be held prisoner or even killed by the Indians. All the crew knew that they were too far from home for help to arrive – even if they could send word of their predicament. And what if Magellan won, but still lost too many men to be able to sail his ship home. And which way would he sail? Would he press on until he finally found the Moluccas?

For 99 days Magellan's crew had sailed without food or fresh water.

Then Magellan was asked to help the King of Cebu. Would he stand and fight and risk the lives of his already exhausted men or would he sail on to the Moluccas?

CAN YOU DECIDE WHAT HAPPENED TO MAGELLAN?

Magellan's men wore armour to protect themselves against attack.

DID MAGELLAN SAIL TO THE MOLUCCAS?

Magellan still had three ships left. It would be possible for some to go on to try to complete the mission and some to go back. But if they did go on they would be sailing an unknown distance in unknown waters. They had only just survived the voyage to Cebu. Next time they might not be so lucky. They might easily run out of food again, die of disease, hit a hidden rock or reef or simply sink in a storm. Everyone knew that Magellan was an expert sailor, but this hadn't helped them before – what if his calculations were wrong and they were miles off course? They had been lucky before, but for how long would their luck hold?

WHAT REALLY HAPPENED TO FERDINAND MAGELLAN?

Magellan died in a skirmish with the Mactan Indians.

Magellan refused to listen to the advice of his officers, attacked Mactan and was killed in the fighting. The King of Cebu then turned against his "allies", killed the two officers chosen to succeed Magellan as joint-commanders and burned one of the ships.

Elcano completed the first voyage around the world, returning to Spain after three years.

ESCAPE TO THE MOLUCCAS

The seamen who survived got away in the two remaining ships and finally did reach the Moluccas. But only one of the ships, *Victoria*, made it all the way back round the tip of Africa – called the "Cape of Good Hope" – to return to Spain. Her commander, a Basque man called Sebastian Elcano, was one of the men who had led the mutiny early on in the voyage.

When they arrived back in Spain in September 1522, almost three years after setting out, the entire crew consisted of 18 Europeans and 4 Indians "weaker than men have ever been before."

Magellan's route proved that the world is indeed round and established a new route to the East.

HONOURING ELCANO

To honour his great achievement, Elcano was allowed to add to his coat of arms a globe and the words "You were the first to encircle me".

It was more than 50 years before another ship went right around the world again. This ship, the *Golden Hind*, was commanded by an Englishman, Sir Francis Drake, and sailed between 1577 and 1580.

A SPANISH CLAIM

As a result of Magellan's expedition, Spain tried to claim the Moluccas but Portugal kept them – paying Spain 350,000 ducats to drop its claim.

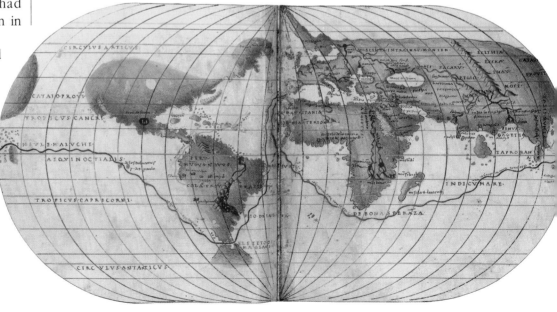

Cortes To Conquer Mexico

(1519)

His Excellency, Diego de Velasquez, the Governor of Cuba, has hereby cancelled the appointment of Hernan Cortes as commander of the planned expedition to Mexico – and ordered his arrest! Has this order come too late? It is said that Cortes and his fleet have already put to sea. No-one knows for certain. And Don Diego is furious.

Hernan Cortes was so determined to command the expedition to Mexico that he used all his savings to help pay for it.

is said that there is a great empire in Mexico, ruled by a people called the Aztecs. Their capital is on an island in a great lake, beyond mountains and jungles, far from the coast. The Aztecs are said to have more gold than a man can imagine – and to worship their gods with human sacrifices. These are travellers' tales. Who knows if they are true?

A MAN ON THE MAKE

Anyone who has met Cortes will know that he is not a man to be stopped when he sets his mind on something. His family was poor but proud. Cortes may have been no more than a hooligan in Spain but he has done well for himself since coming to the Indies. He fought bravely in Cuba and has been rewarded with an estate. He also has a fine house in Santiago and has served there as mayor.

RESTLESS AND RUTHLESS

When Don Diego offered him the Mexico command he jumped at it. Cortes

seems to have been running out of control from the start – behaving as though it was his expedition and not the governor's. He has recruited 300 men and six ships in just a month. Who can say what he has promised them?

WHAT WILL HE FIND?

If Cortes has given the Governor the slip, what has he let his men in for? It

The Aztecs were a superstitious people who worshipped many gods. This is Coatlicue, the goddess of life and death.

Central and South America were rumoured to be rich in gold, and many European explorers travelled there to search for it.

BRAVE CORTES SETS

By the time Cortes sailed for Mexico in February 1519 he had collected 11 ships, 500 soldiers and 100 sailors. Most were armed with swords, some had crossbows, a few even had guns - and there were 16 horses. When Cortes landed in Mexico he burned his fleet. Everyone knew that there was no going back. They had two choices - victory or death.

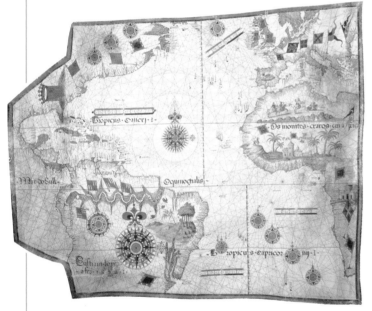

Explorers tried to keep detailed maps of the areas they visited, increasing our knowledge of the world.

FINDING A TONGUE

Cortes had an amazing stroke of luck when some local Indians gave him a captured princess as a present. She spoke the Aztec language, Nahuatl.

Cortes soon saw she was very clever and knew a lot about the Aztecs. She became his interpreter and adviser. The Spaniards called her Lady Marina but the Aztecs came to call her 'Malinche' – 'tongue' – because Cortes always spoke through her.

MR. MAYOR

Cortes knew that some of his men were still worrying that he had disobeyed Don Diego, so he got them to build a little town, called Vera Cruz – True Cross. The men elected Cortes as Mayor. As Mayor of a Spanish town Cortes could deal directly with the King of Spain and didn't need to take orders from the Governor of a colony such as Cuba.

GOLD FOR A GOD

Cortes sent a message to the Aztec emperor, Moctezuma, saying that the Spanish had a sickness which only gold could cure. The Aztecs were not sure what to make of the newcomers. They had never seen or heard of anything like their ships and guns and swords and horses. Perhaps they were gods from the sky? They sent Cortes presents of gold – but tried to keep him away from their capital by telling him that the journey through the mountains would be impossible.

FINDING ALLIES

Malinche told Cortes that the Aztecs were hated by many of the tribes in their empire. They made them pay heavy taxes and work as slaves and give them 50,000 young men and women every year to kill as sacrifices.

Many Indians offered to join Cortes and fight the Aztecs. On 16 August 1519, with 400 of his own men and 300 Indians, Cortes set off to march on the Aztec capital, Tenochtitlan. As they passed from steaming jungles to icy mountains Cortes and his men picked

Cortes and his men found many beautiful and strange things, such as this turquoise and shell mask thought to represent Quetzacoatl – the Aztec god of wind, learning and priesthood.

SAILS FOR MEXICO!

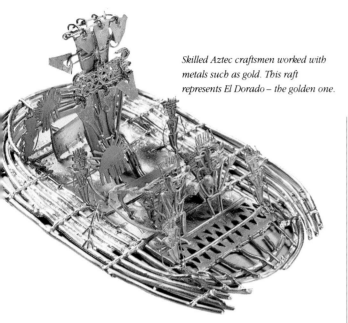

Skilled Aztec craftsmen worked with metals such as gold. This raft represents El Dorado – the golden one.

up thousands more Indian allies – and defeated any who would not join them.

TURNING THE TABLES

By the time Cortes reached the Aztec capital,

Moctezuma had heard that he was a great warrior. He welcomed Cortes as an honoured guest and gave him piles of gold and a royal palace to live in. A few days after his arrival Cortes simply arrested Moctezuma and started

giving orders in his name. When a group of Aztecs killed some of his men Cortes had them burned alive – and Moctezuma approved!

Then came news from the coast. A force of Spaniards, sent by Don Diego, had landed at Vera Cruz – with orders to arrest Cortes!

The Aztecs built their magnificent capital city, Tenochtitlan, on an island in Lake Texcoco.

Aztecs believed that their gods needed gifts to feed them and stop them destroying the world. The most important gift was a human sacrifice. These were carried out at the vast temple complex in Tenochtitlan.

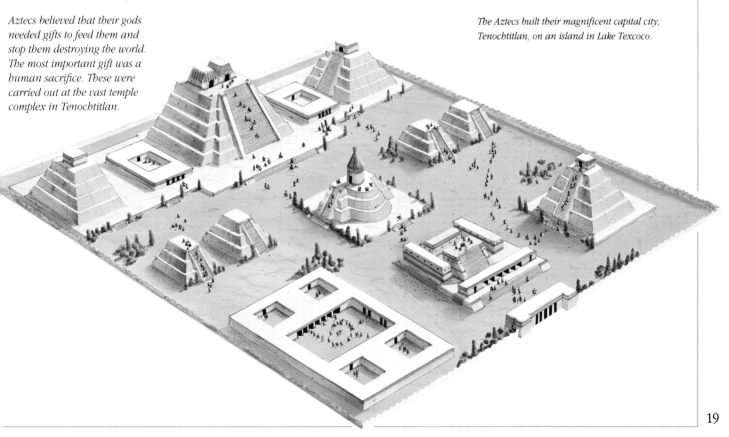

The Spanish were all well armed and would prove an even match for Cortes and his men. They also knew the importance of defending themselves and wore armour and helmets such as this morion helmet.

HERNAN CORTES

WHAT HAPPENED NEXT?

DID CORTES FIGHT THE NEWCOMERS?

The Aztec empire covered an area as big as Italy. Would two groups of a few hundred men be sure to find each other? Surely it was just as likely that either or both parties might just get lost? Maybe they would be attacked by local Indian tribes before they even got close to one another?

Don Diego's men had only just landed and were not used to the country. They might fall sick and die from an Indian disease. Or they might not be able to find food and simply starve to death?

DID CORTES BEAT THE NEWCOMERS?

Suppose that Cortes did find the Spanish expeditionary force. Did he fight and beat them? Perhaps he even showed them the gold he had got and persuaded them to join him.

What then? He had burned all of his ships so he and his men were stranded there. Would he take over the ships they had come in and sail back to Cuba? or even to Spain? Then he could talk to the King direct and ask for a whole army to help him conquer Mexico for good.

Or would he turn back and try to take control of Tenochtitlan again? If he tried this, would his men follow him?

And, after a battle, would there be enough fit men left to start another fight for Tenochtitlan or sail back to Spain?

Cortes had had control of Tenochtitlan and had sold the Aztecs into slavery. If he had to fight the Spaniards, would Cortes still be able to control the Aztecs?

WAS CORTES KILLED BY THE SPANIARDS?

Suppose Cortes and his men were allowed to leave Tenochtitlan, perhaps taking Moctezuma with them. They would then have to go back through the mountains to face a force of fresh men who might well outnumber them and who were quite possibly much better armed. And suppose that the commander of this force offered a free pardon to Cortes' men if they would come over to his side? Would they stick by him and fight? And, if they did, would they win? What if Cortes was killed by the Spaniards? What would his men do then?

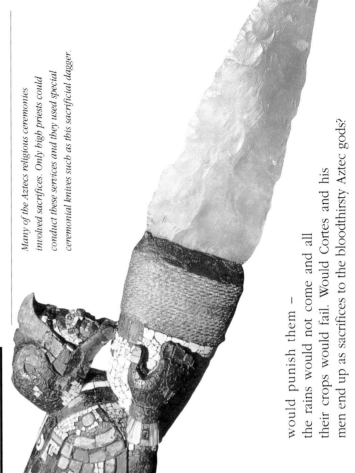

Many of the Aztecs religious ceremonies involved sacrifices. Only high priests could conduct these services and they used special ceremonial knives such as this sacrificial dagger.

Cortes and his men had taken over the Aztec capital Tenochtitlan.

But Don Diego had sent his men to arrest Cortes. Would Cortes be able to fight Don Diego's men and still control Tenochtitlan?

WHAT DO YOU THINK HAPPENED TO CORTES?

Cortes and his men could have teamed up with the local Indians to fight the new Spaniards.

WAS CORTES KILLED BY THE AZTECS?

Cortes and his men were surrounded by a million Aztecs. He did hold Moctezuma as a hostage – but after agreeing to having his own people killed, the Aztecs might decide that Moctezuma had betrayed them and was just a worthless puppet. Cortes also had Indian allies – but they might still be afraid of the Aztecs and desert him. Or they might decide that the Aztecs were too weak to rule them any more and just go home.

But what would happen if the Aztecs captured them? Cortes was well aware of what the Aztecs did to their prisoners. They sacrificed them to their gods. The Aztecs believed that the gods needed sacrifices for nourishment. Without this nourishment, the gods would punish them – the rains would not come and all their crops would fail. Would Cortes and his men end up as sacrifices to the bloodthirsty Aztec gods?

WHAT REALLY HAPPENED TO HERNAN CORTES?

The Spanish tried to convert the Aztecs to Christianity, celebrating Mass after battles.

Cortes left a hundred men behind in Tenochtitlan and marched the rest to Vera Cruz so quickly that he was able to ambush the newcomers by night and force them to surrender. He then persuaded many of them to join him and they went back to Tenochtitlan, where they were allowed back into the city.

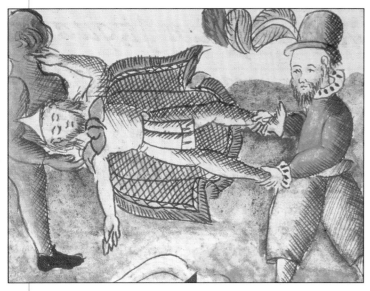

The Aztecs felt Moctezuma had betrayed them, so they killed him.

TRAPPED!

What Cortes and his men did not realise was that the Aztecs had only allowed them back in to trap them. The Aztec chiefs saw Moctezuma as a traitor and chose his brother, Cuitlahuac, as their leader instead. Now they attacked Cortes and his men in every way they could. When Moctezuma was sent out to speak to them they stoned him to death.

On the night of 30 June 1520 Cortes and his men fought their way out of the lake-city and on to the shore. Hundreds of them were killed in the retreat

RAISING A NEW ARMY

Cortes raised a huge new army of Indian allies and built a fleet of 13 ships.

Meanwhile Cuitlahuac died of smallpox – which he had somehow caught from the Spanish. Cortes besieged Tenochtitlan by land and sea until its defenders, weakened by starvation and smallpox, surrendered.

Then he destroyed the city completely and built a new capital on its ruins. It is now Mexico City.

BUILDING UP THE EMPIRE

Cortes sent out expeditions to add the areas which are now Guatemala and El Salvador to the new Spanish empire. But the government in Spain was afraid that Cortes wanted to set himself up as king. Officials were sent to take over running the country. Cortes went back to Spain to ask that he should be confirmed as Governor of Mexico. He was treated with great respect – but he was not made Governor. Cortes spent his last years in Spain, a forgotten hero.

Cortes died in poverty in Spain. Few monuments exist to honour him, but this can be found in the Chapultepec Palace in Mexico.

FORGOTTEN IN MEXICO?

When Cortes died in 1547 his body was shipped back to Mexico City for burial. But in all of Mexico there are only a few statues of Cortes to this day.

Cook to Explore the Pacific

1768

Experts are expressing surprise at the appointment of forty-year-old James Cook to command a major scientific expedition. He will explore the South Seas and visit Tahiti to make astronomical observations as the planet Venus crosses the face of the sun.

Cook's first goal was to set up an observatory on the island of Tahiti.

James Cook was one of the world's greatest navigators.

THE NAVY INSISTS

The expedition is a joint effort by Britain's Royal Navy and the Royal Society, Europe's leading scientific institution. It is well known that the Royal Society wished to appoint the brilliant young Mr. Alexander Dalrymple as leader. He has made a great reputation charting routes to China for the trading ships of the East India Company, and is an accomplished geographer and astronomer. But the Royal Navy insists that command of their ship must be given to a serving officer, not a civilian.

THE MAN FROM NOWHERE

James Cook is not what most people would call a typical career officer. He has made his way to the top purely on merit. He was born the son of a common labourer and is self-taught as a navigator. After working in a grocer's shop he first went to sea in a ship carrying coal from Newcastle to London but gave up a very promising future to enlist in the Navy as an ordinary seaman. Within two years he was master of his own ship.

Cook's skill in charting the treacherous waters of the St. Lawrence River was decisive in helping British forces capture the French-held city of Quebec in 1759. Since then he has spent his time surveying the coasts of eastern Canada and Newfoundland.

No-one doubts Cook's courage or skill, but can he command the respect of 11 scientists as well as 80 sailors?

IS THIS THE RIGHT SHIP?

Cook's choice of ship has caused as much comment as his appointment. Rather than a regular ship of the line, he has picked out a coal-ship of the sort he served on as a youth. Critics say she looks more sturdy than stylish – rather like Cook himself. Certainly she has enough room to carry all the stores needed for such a long voyage – but will a vessel built for sailing in coastal waters be capable of going right around the world? She has been re-named *Endeavour,* perhaps because Cook knows she will have to try hard.

James Cook drew detailed charts showing the coastline and position of islands on his voyages. This one shows the passage from Cape Torment into the south channels of Orleans.

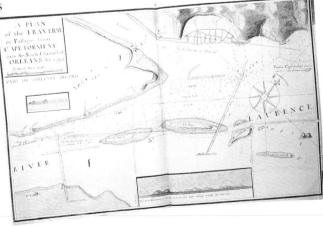

1769

Cook insisted that his men drink orange and lemon juice, and eat carrot marmalade to prevent scurvy.

Endeavour left Plymouth on 25 August 1768 and, after calling at Madeira and Rio de Janeiro, rounded Cape Horn without trouble in fine weather, reaching Tahiti on 10 April 1769, seven months later.

THE DREADED SCURVY

Normally on a voyage of such length it was expected that several men would die of scurvy, and many more would be suffering from its first signs, such as loose teeth and blotchy skin. No one was as yet quite sure what scurvy was, whether it was one disease or several, or what caused it. Learned doctors thought it was due to the wrong sort of diet, although they disagreed about how it could be prevented. Just to make sure Cook forced his men to drink orange and lemon juice, swallow doses of molasses and eat vegetable soups, pickled cabbage and carrot marmalade. Thanks to these measures not one man died on the voyage to Tahiti.

A SHORT STAY IN PARADISE

Cook's men received a friendly welcome in Tahiti and the astronomers were able to set up their temporary observatory without difficulty. The passage of Venus across the sun was recorded on 3 June 1769 according to plan. The only problem with the native people was that they kept stealing anything made of iron, which they had never seen before and thought was wonderful.

Sailors used a sextant to measure the angle between two objects in the sky, such as stars, and were then able to calculate their position.

▶ 10 April 1769   Cook reaches Tahiti.
▶ 1769–1770   Cook circumnavigate
                  New Zealand.
▶ 21 April 1770   Cook makes landfall
                  Botany Bay
▶ 12 July 1770   runs aground on the
                  Great Barrier Reef.

NEW GUINEA

INDONESIA

GREA
BARR
REEF

AUSTRALIA

BOTANY
BAY

TASM
SEA

250   500   miles

400   800   km

SCALE

INDIAN OCEAN

PICKLED CABBAGE

Maori warriors attacked Cook and his men when they landed on the east coast of New Zealand.

SECRET ORDERS TO GO SOUTH

After leaving Tahiti, Cook opened his secret orders telling him to sail south and find out if there was a southern continent – Terra Australis Incognita.

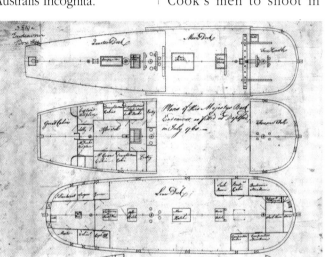

The Endeavour *was completely refitted before Cook sailed to Tahiti. New cabins were built and the underplanking was reinforced to protect against shipworm.*

Cook did as instructed, but found nothing but empty seas. He turned his ship and sailed west until he landed on the east coast of New Zealand. Here Maori warriors attacked them, forcing Cook's men to shoot in self-defence and kill three of them.

Cook then sailed a figure-of-eight course to prove that New Zealand was two separate islands and not part of the supposed lost southern continent.

WHICH WAY HOME?

Cook was now free to return home, either eastwards back round Cape Horn, or westwards round the Cape of Good Hope. He chose to go west as this would allow him to explore the eastern coast of New Holland, as Australia was then called.

On 21 April 1770 Cook reached the south-eastern tip of Australia and turned north, charting the coast as he went, until he anchored where his scientists found so many plants that they called it Botany Bay. They also found dart-throwing aborigines and were glad to move on.

Cook thought the countryside reminded him of a part of Britain and called it New South Wales. He claimed it as British territory and recorded in his journal that it would be a good place for a colony.

Sailing ever northwards Cook gradually found himself being pushed closer to the shore as the distance between it and the Great Barrier Reef of coral off-shore grew narrower. Suddenly, on the night of 11 July came a sickening crunch and *Endeavour* shook from end to end as she crashed onto a submerged section of the reef and stuck fast...

What would happen to the ship and her crew?...

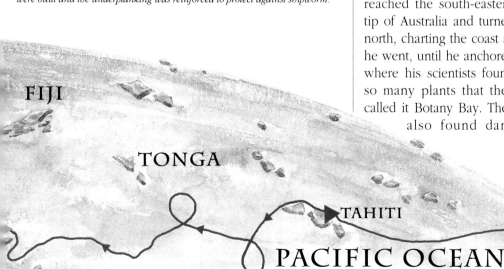

FIJI

TONGA

TAHITI

PACIFIC OCEAN

EW ALAND

N
W — E
S

Coral reefs are made up of the skeletons of tiny invertebrate animals. Their strong, sharp surfaces can damage ships.

CAPTAIN COOK

WHAT HAPPENED NEXT?

DID ENDEAVOUR NEED REPAIRS?

*E*ndeavour had been at sea for almost two years without a refit and had sailed through extremes of temperatures, both hot and cold. What damage might have been done before the crash and gone unnoticed?

Suppose *Endeavour* could be freed from the reef but was too badly damaged to sail on without repairs. Did Cook's men have the skills and materials to do this? They would have to beach *Endeavour* on the shore. This would mean they might be attacked by aborigines, frightened by these strange newcomers. What if they were outnumbered? Suppose the aborigines were defeated the first time, would they come back with reinforcements?

them almost two years to get there. How long would it be before anyone realised they were in trouble and sent help? How many crew would there be when the rescue ship finally arrived? Would anyone live to tell the tale?

threw these away, how would they protect themselves if they were attacked? Ships travelling on such long voyages were very carefully packed, as space was always a problem, so they only carried the bare minimum of supplies. Whatever they threw away would surely be needed, and would they be able to get by without it?

COULD ENDEAVOUR FLOAT OFF THE REEF?

Suppose *Endeavour* was not completely stuck but was just held there while the tide turned. When the high tide came, would it be possible to float the ship off the reef and continue the voyage? If the crew threw everything that wasn't absolutely vital for survival over-board, would this make here light enough to float?

But such drastic action might mean that they would not be able to complete their mission – to chart the coast of Australia and claim the land for Britain. Without Cook's navigational equipment it would be impossible to draw the charts accurately, and it would also be impossible to find their way home. These must surely be counted as essential items. So what else could be thrown over-board?

Food barrels and oil jars could easily be discarded, but would they then have enough to eat? The cannons and guns were certainly heavy, but if they

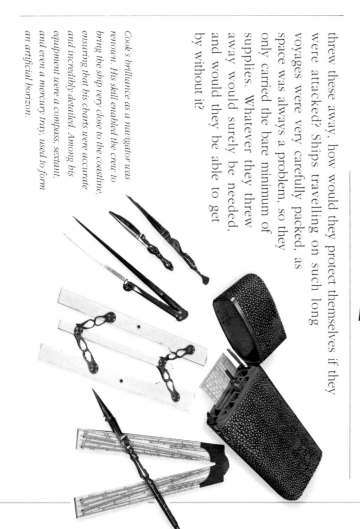

Cook's brilliance as a navigator was renown. His skill enabled the crew to bring the ship very close to the coastline, ensuring that his charts were accurate and incredibly detailed. Among his equipment were a compass, sextant, and even a mercury tray, used to form an artificial horizon.

26

Cook thought that scurvy was caused by the lack of fresh food. He gave his crew fresh fruit and vegetables whenever they were available, even though much of this was unfamiliar and strange tasting, like this breadfruit

picked up in an area that was completely unknown to Europeans. Or maybe it was just coincidence that all the crew had remained healthy, and the fresh fruit was really not helping at all – would they all become ill and die many miles from home?

Suppose all the crew came down with an unknown illness. Would there be enough healthy men left to sail the ship? What if they found themselves in the middle of the ocean with only a few healthy men and no way home?

WAS ENDEAVOUR STUCK?

Even if hitting a coral reef did no major damage to a ship it might still leave *Endeavour* stuck fast. Cook and his men were thousands of miles from the nearest possible help. If they failed to refloat her what else could they do but abandon her and go ashore. And then? Would the local people be friendly or would Cook and his men have to fight them? Cook's crew had guns, and even cannons on board *Endeavour*, but no-one knew what kind of weapons the locals might have. And they were 12,000 miles from England. It had taken

---

The *Endeavour* had been at sea for almost two years. Originally she had been built as a coal-ship, designed to carry coal in the North Sea.

Had it been a mistake to take this ship so far from home?

CAN YOU DECIDE WHAT HAPPENED TO THE *ENDEAVOUR*?

Among Cook's crew were two carpenters. It was their job to repair the ship in the event of an accident. This is a replica of the Endeavour, built in honour of the 200th anniversary of the Australian nation.

Cook used this cutlery while on the Endeavour. He insisted people should eat as varied a diet as possible. He tried keeping hens and sheep on board to give a supply of fresh eggs and meat.

DID THEY DIE OF DISEASE?

Cook was very strict about keeping his crew clean and healthy. He insisted that every member of the crew wash at least once a week and they had to change their clothing twice a week. He attached great importance to a healthy diet, giving everyone fresh meat, vegetables and fruit whenever he could. Certainly this seemed to be working as no-one had succumbed to the deadly disease, scurvy, but would these measures be effective against unknown illnesses

WHAT REALLY HAPPENED TO CAPTAIN JAMES COOK?

By skilful seamanship, and after a tremendous struggle, Cook and his men managed to refloat his ship and beach her at the mouth of what is now called Endeavour River, near to modern-day Cooktown. Even though weeks were spent repairing her hull, *Endeavour* was still leaking when Cook edged her outside the Barrier Reef – only to escape drifting on to it again by seconds as a sudden change of breeze saved him from certain disaster.

Captain James Cook was killed by Hawaiian warriors on 14 February 1779. The expedition then returned to England.

Hawaiian warriors were often armed with clubs and spears.

SHIPWRECKED AGAIN?

Yet another near-shipwreck occurred before *Endeavour* finally limped into the Dutch-held port of Batavia in October 1770. Here further repairs were made and, despite all his careful precautions, the crew were exposed to such well-known killer-diseases as malaria and dysentery while on land. Four officers and 26 of the men were to die before *Endeavour* finally reached England in July 1771.

TWO MORE EXPEDITIONS

Cook went on to command two more expeditions to the South Seas. He became the first navigator to cross the Antarctic Circle and did finally prove that there was no great undiscovered southern continent. He was also the first European to visit the Cook Islands and the Sandwich Islands and to show that there was no North-West Passage to link the Pacific and the Atlantic Oceans.

In January 1779, during the course of his third voyage, Cook called at Hawaii to repair his ships. The local chiefs and priests treated him like a god and made their people give him and his men many feasts and gifts. When Cook finally left they were secretly glad to see him go because they had so little food left. Two days later a broken foremast forced Cook to return.

Soon after he landed there were quarrels between his crew and the local people. Cook, the master-navigator and accomplished sailor, was stabbed and clubbed to death in a scuffle over a stolen boat.

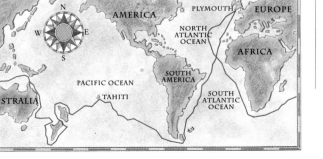

James Cook surveyed thousands of kilometres of coastline and improved our knowledge of the Pacific Ocean.

Has Franklin Found It?

1845

Sir John Franklin has been the victim of a vile whispering campaign, put about by dogs – we can scarcely call them men – who would not dare to whine their insults to his face. And of what is he accused? He is accused of the crime of being 59 years of age. Far too old, they say, to command the most important Arctic expedition of our age.

John Franklin faced resistance over his appointment to command the expedition to find a North-West passage.

who landed the first ship to survive an entire winter in Arctic waters? What does Parry say of Franklin? "He is a fitter man to go than any I know." We really must appreciate the talent we have. Let the whispering stop. Let Franklin go.

TOO OLD?

Have they never heard of experience? Sir John Franklin has served in Her Majesty's Navy for 45 years! He saw action at the age of 15! He was with Lord Nelson at Trafalgar! And he has been taking part in polar expeditions for some 30 years! Is all this experience to count for nothing! Whose opinions are we to trust? Those of the people who whisper their poison in dark corners? Or that of Admiral Sir Edward Parry,

Martin Frobisher was the first explorer to search for a North-West passage.

A BRITISH ROUTE

For over 250 years sailors have been searching for a North-West passage through Arctic waters. Franklin's route will take him through the icy wastes of British North America – icy, but British!

This chart showing the frozen waters of the Arctic was drawn by James Wyld.

THE BEST-EQUIPPED EVER TO LEAVE

1846

Sir John Franklin's aim was defined by the Admiralty as *"the discovery of a North-West Passage, only a small part of which is still unknown."* He was ordered to sail into Baffin Bay, enter Lancaster Sound and pass through Barrow Strait, until he came to Cape Walker – *"Thence he is to steer to the southward and westward towards Bering Strait, in as straight a line as is permitted by ice or any unknown land."* This was not the route that Franklin wished to follow.

SETTING SAIL

The expedition sailed from the River Thames on 18 May 1845. It was last seen north of Baffin Island at the entrance to Lancaster Sound on 25 or 26 July of that year.

HMS Erebus *and* HMS Terror *sailing through the frozen waters.*

THE RIGHT SHIPS

HMS Erebus (370 tons) and *HMS Terror* (340 tons) have already proved themselves in Antarctic waters, having been used on previous expeditions there! They have been specially adapted to face the worst that ice can do. Each ship is encased in iron at the bow and for 20 feet along each side. Steam-engines adapted from the Greenwich railway have been fitted to provide extra power. Each engine can generate a power equal to that of 20 horses! and can – without the aid of sails – propel the vessel forward at speeds of up to four miles an hour! Every consideration has been given to the comfort and warmth of the hand-picked crew. Their blankets are made of the skins of wolves and their cabins are heated by an ingenious system of pipes which circulate hot water through them!

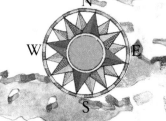

BATHURST ISLAND

BEECHEY ISLAND

SOMERSET ISLAND

PRINCE OF WALES ISLAND

VICTORIA ISLAND

FRANKLIN STRAIT

BOOTHIA PENINSULAR

KING WILLIAM ISLAND

N
W E
S

ARCTIC EXPEDITION
BRITISH SHORES

The Cross of the Order of Hanover was awarded to Franklin by William IV.

NOURISHING THE BODY...

The brave men of the Franklin expedition can be sure of a sound diet to keep them fit and cheerful. The stores carried by the expedition have been chosen with the best advice of Britain's most experienced explorers and most learned scientists. They include over half a ton of raisins and more than four tons of chocolate to provide concentrated energy. Four tons of lemon juice have also been included to prevent scurvy.

No expense has been spared in taking advantage of the huge advances in science which are so much a feature of our times. Each ship's stores contain thousands of tins of canned foods – rich soups, prime meat and excellent vegetables. Using a technology pioneered for the Royal Navy, the suppliers have ensured that each can is made entirely airtight against decay with a lead seal.

...AND THE SOUL

Everyone will know that, as an outstanding Christian, Sir John has taken every care for the souls as well as the bodies of his men. He had planned to have copies of the Bible to sell at cost price but so many have been donated by well-wishers that this has not proved necessary. Each ship however carries supplies of slates, paper and pencils so that unlettered seamen can use their off-duty hours to learn to read and write. Those who can already do so can take advantage of the fine library of 1,200 books which is carried aboard each ship.

This chronometer watch was issued to HMS Terror for the voyage.

THE WIFE WHO WAITS

Every heart must go out to Lady Jane Franklin, the gracious wife of the gallant commander. Will he return in time to celebrate the 20th anniversary of their wedding in triumph as a national hero?... ***Or are Franklin and his crew lost forever?...***

Lady Jane Franklin was the devoted wife and companion of Sir John Franklin.

GREENLAND

DEVON ISLAND

LANCASTER SOUND

MELVILLE BAY

BAFFIN BAY

BAFFIN ISLAND

Entering Lancaster Sound

Circumnavigates Bathurst Island

Successfully navigates Franklin Strait

Reaches King William Island

Navigation was not always reliable in extreme temperatures.

DID THE SHIPS SINK?

The simplest explanation was that the ships had been sunk by a storm or an iceberg or crushed by pack ice. If this had happened, there might be no trace of either ship or of the men.

DID FRANKLIN AND HIS MEN FALL SICK?

Only the fittest men had been chosen for the voyage, but long sea voyages were notorious for damaging men's health. Lemon juice and pickled vegetables had been packed to prevent scurvy, but what about other diseases? The ships had medical supplies, but would there be enough medicine to cure everyone if they got sick?

Supposing there were an outbreak of an infectious disease such as typhus? Typhus, which is carried by fleas, had destroyed Napoleon's army in the fierce Russian winter back in 1812. The fleas – and therefore the disease – spread easily among men huddled close together against the cold. And it was almost always fatal. Even if some men survived an epidemic, there might be too few to work the ship, leaving them stranded in the frozen waters.

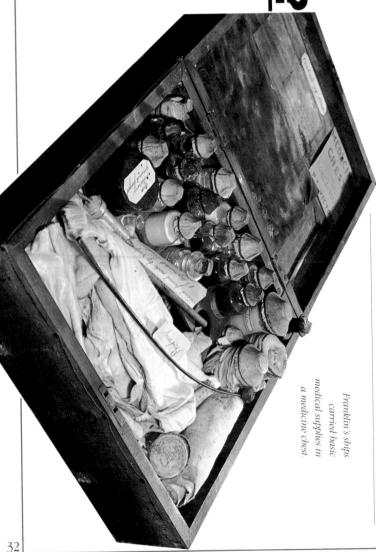

Franklin's ships carried basic medical supplies in a medicine chest.

SIR JOHN FRANKLIN

WHAT HAPPENED NEXT?

DID FRANKLIN STARVE?

The expedition had packed enough stores for three years. With hunting and fishing, the supplies might even last for five. But some of the crew had written to their wives that they might be away for up to six years. And supposing the food had gone rotten?

Surely this wouldn't be a problem in subzero Arctic temperatures. But the temperature in the ships wasn't subzero – they were heated. And the crews, being so closely packed together, would generate body heat. Perhaps, too, this new fangled method of preserving food in cans wasn't all that reliable. If the food supply failed, what would the crew do?

New technology enabled people to seal foods in cans – making them ideal for long sea voyages.

WERE THEY POISONED?

This is not a theory that occurred to anyone at the time. But a great deal of the expedition's food – meat, soups, vegetables – was stored in lead-sealed cans. Food was often eaten off plates with a lead glaze or made of pewter, a mixture of tin and lead. Drinks were taken from lead-glazed and pewter jugs and cups. Lead was used in making the medicines and ointments used by the crew and also in the paints with which both ships were painted. We now know that everyday use of products containing lead can cause a dangerous and even fatal buildup of lead in the human body. The very fact that this was not known in Franklin's day meant that nobody would have suspected what was happening if people had gotten ill from lead poisoning – or how to treat it even if they had known.

Franklin had taken particular care over his preparations for the voyage. *The ships had already been tested in the severe Antarctic weather, but could they survive another arduous voyage?*

WHAT DO YOU THINK HAPPENED TO FRANKLIN?

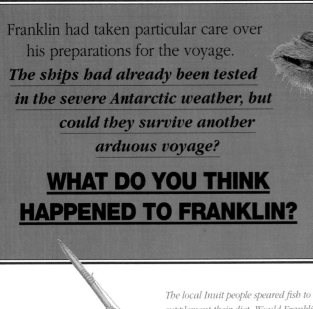

The local Inuit people speared fish to supplement their diet. Would Franklin and his men be able to do this?

DID THEY FREEZE TO DEATH?

Franklin was sailing farther north than anyone had ever attempted before. Suppose his careful preparations simply weren't good enough? Suppose the ingenious hot-water heating system for the cabins failed? Or perhaps the crews had managed to keep warm enough and the ships themselves had got frozen permanently in the ice?

We now know that the Arctic weather in the 1840s was even worse than it is today. In fact, the weather in the 1840s was probably the worst ever in the 700 years for which there is some sort of record.

The Inuits wore clothes of seal fur to help them survive in the freezing weather. Did Franklin and his men have enough warm clothes?

WHAT REALLY HAPPENED TO SIR JOHN FRANKLIN?

John Torrington's body was found in 1981. An investigation revealed he had died from lead poisoning. He died on January 1st 1846, aged 20 years.

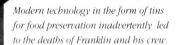

Thirty-two expeditions were sent to find out what had happened to Franklin and his men. In 1859 Leopold McClintock, leader of an expedition paid for by Lady Franklin, finally found several skeletons and a written account of what had happened up to 25 April 1848.

ICE-BOUND

Both Franklin's ships the *HMS Erebus* and the *HMS Terror* had become ice-bound in September 1846 and been carried for miles in the pack ice.

ABANDONED SHIPS

After Franklin himself and 24 other men had died, it was decided in April 1848 to abandon the ships and, using the ship's boats, try to sail and march south to the Canadian mainland.

Tragically, everyone died before reaching safety. The *Erebus* and the *Terror* were crushed by the ice and finally sank without trace.

Modern technology in the form of tins for food preservation inadvertently led to the deaths of Franklin and his crew.

THE LATEST EVIDENCE

In 1981, Canadian archaeologists discovered the body of John Torrington, a young sailor of Franklin's crew. Laboratory tests on his bones showed that he had ten times the normal level of lead in his body. As yet, there is not enough evidence to say what caused this or whether other crew members also suffered – and possibly even died – from lead-poisoning.

THE ARCTIC LEGACY

In 1944, a Canadian 'Mountie', Sargeant Larsen, managed to sail through the North-West Passage in a single summer. In modern times, both American and Russian ice breakers have forced their way through the passage several times. But the weather conditions have always been too severe for this ever to become a regular route for shipping.

Lady Franklin commissioned a ship called The Fox *to search for her missing husband.*

Amundsen and Scott Both Head South!

1908

Sailing in his Nansen's own ship, Fram, Amundsen set off for the South Pole.

It has been reported from Madeira that the Norwegian expedition headed by Roald Amundsen is not bound for the Arctic as originally announced - but to the Antarctic! Amundsen wanted to be the first man to reach the North Pole, but the American Robert Peary has beaten him to it. So he's heading south!

A British expedition, led by naval captain Robert Falcon Scott, is already on its way to Antarctica, with the aim of getting a team to the South Pole. Is this going to turn into a race?

AMUNDSEN – NO AMATEUR

When it comes to a polar exploration Amundsen is 100 per cent dedicated. Ever since boyhood his heroes have been the Englishman, Franklin, and his fellow-countryman Nansen, who was the first man to cross Greenland's ice-fields. As a youth Amundsen slept with his bedroom window open throughout the Norwegian winter to harden himself to the cold. A brilliant skier, he has set himself to master every skill an explorer could need. It is generally admitted that the Belgian Antarctic expedition of 1897-9 would have been a total disaster if Amundsen hadn't taken over. Between 1903 and 1906 he succeeded where his hero, Franklin, had failed and sailed right through the North-West passage. Now he has Nansen's own ship, *Fram*, and he is heading south. Can anyone doubt what his aim is?

Amundsen was 38 years old when he set off to reach the South Pole.

was 13. His father, grandfather and great-grandfather were all sailors. Between 1901 and 1904 he led the National Antarctic Expedition which explored Victoria Land and Edward VII Land. During the course of one sledging journey Scott and two companions, Wilson and Shackleton, went further south than anyone had ever been before. He is now determined to become the first man to reach the South Pole itself.

In 1908 Shackleton led another expedition to within 100 miles of the South Pole. An English route has therefore been mapped out and it seems only fitting that an Englishman should finish the job.

AN ENGLISHMAN CALLED SCOTT

Captain Scott has been in the Royal Navy since he

The South Pole had yet to be reached. Other expeditions had tried and failed – but who will succeed?

Scott was determined that an Englishman would reach the South Pole first.

35

1910

SCOTT

Scott's ship, the ex-whaler *Terra Nova*, sailed from England on 15 June 1910. When he arrived in New Zealand to stock up with fresh supplies Scott learned that Amundsen was also on his way to the South Pole.

Scott was determined not to change his own plans. He established winter quarters at Cape

AMUNDSEN

Amundsen had set sail from Norway on 7 June 1910. After leaving Madeira he sailed straight for the Antarctic and in January 1911 set up a base-camp, 'Framheim', about 60 miles nearer the South Pole than Scott's camp was. On 4 February the Norwegians were visited by *Terra Nova*, commanded in

Scott's absence by Lt. Campbell. There was no bad feeling between the two groups but Campbell decided it would be better to stay clear of the Norwegians and changed his plans so that the *Terra Nova* party would explore South Victoria Land, rather

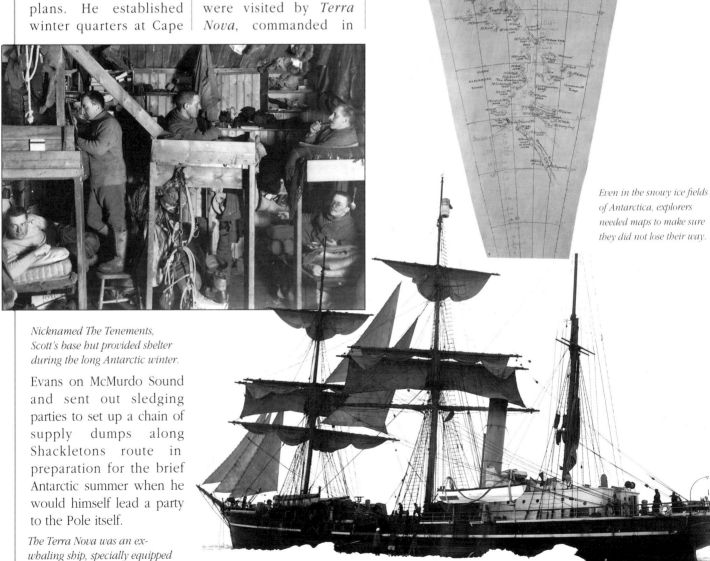

Even in the snowy ice fields of Antarctica, explorers needed maps to make sure they did not lose their way.

Nicknamed The Tenements, Scott's base hut provided shelter during the long Antarctic winter.

Evans on McMurdo Sound and sent out sledging parties to set up a chain of supply dumps along Shackletons route in preparation for the brief Antarctic summer when he would himself lead a party to the Pole itself.

The Terra Nova was an ex-whaling ship, specially equipped for the voyage.

O THE POLE.
HERE FIRST?

The base camp provided a warm haven from the extreme weather.

than Edward VII Land as originally intended. Shortly afterwards *Fram* sailed off on a scientific cruise in warmer waters to the north.

From February until April Amundsen and his men did what Scott and his men were doing and laid a chain of supply dumps which they could use when they set out for the Pole itself when the weather was most favourable.

Then both groups settled in their huts to sit out the Antarctic winter.

SCOTT

Scott set out for the South Pole on 24 October 1911. His party was equipped with motorised tractor-sledges, plus ponies and dogs. They felt fit to face any eventuality, having plenty of supplies for the animals and themselves.

AMUNDSEN

Desperate to beat Scott, Amundsen tried to set out in late August.

But the intense cold forced Amundsen and his men to turn back and recover at their base camp. They did not set off again until 15 October.

Will both parties reach the Pole?... And who will get there first?...

In the extreme cold, every action demanded extra effort. Scott and his men used ponies to help pull the heavy sledges, saving their own energy.

Amundsen called his base camp Framheim. Supplies of food and extra equipment could be stored here.

Scott's team were following a route that had been pioneered by Shackleton. But would this give them an advantage?

DID AMUNDSEN GET THERE FIRST?

A mundsen was determined to beat Scott. He had set his base camp 60 miles nearer the South Pole than Scott's was. He had much more experience of polar exploration than Scott. Scott had more or less drifted into the business of exploration. Amundsen had never wanted to do anything else. He and his men were all expert skiers and superbly fit. With ten dogs for every man they would surely have enough pulling power to overcome any obstacle they might meet.

Amundsen and his men were all well trained and fully equipped for their journey. But they had trained to go to the North Pole – would their skills help them at the South Pole?

WHAT HAPPENED NEXT?

DID BOTH PARTIES GET THERE?

B oth parties had planned as well as they knew how. But both were up against the possibility that a severe blizzard could totally wreck their plans. Amundsen had already been forced to turn back once by the sheer intensity of the cold. A blizzard could kill a party outright if they couldn't get into their tents in time. Or it could bury them alive. Or it could delay them so long that they would run out of food before they got to their next supply-dump. And there was always the possibility of an accident or illness. Suppose one or more

A lthough he started out later than Amundsen and from farther away, Scott did have the advantage of following a route which had already been pioneered for almost the entire distance by Shackleton. And he knew what hazards to expect as he had been with Shackleton on the earlier mission.

Scott also had three different kinds of transport to rely on – ponies, tractor-sledges and dogs, whereas Amundsen was risking everything on his dog-teams. If the dog-teams proved unsuitable, Scott would be able to press on with one of his other forms of transport, while Amundsen would be forced to carry all his equipment.

High-calorie foods such as these blocks of Bovril provided the explorers with the energy they needed.

"BOVRIL" PEMMICAN.

DID THEY RUN OUT OF FOOD?

W hat if all the careful preparations had gone wrong and they simply didn't have enough to eat? They needed a high-calorie diet to withstand the extreme cold. Severe weather could keep them in their camps for several days – maybe even weeks – and if they ran low on food, would they have enough strength to continue the journey?

Both Amundsen and Scott were experienced explorers, and both were determined to reach the South Pole first.

Scott had not expected to have to race – but would his prior knowledge of the area give him the advantage over Amundsen

WHO DO YOU THINK
GOT THERE FIRST?

men, perhaps through carelessness, developed frost-bite or had a bad fall and broke a leg. Would the whole group have to turn back? Or, in such a case, would the leader decide to split his party, sending some back with the casualty and going on to the Pole with the rest? If this happened, how would it affect the carefully planned rationing of supplies?

The explorers could only take what they could carry, so Scott and his men used sledges to drag their heavy loads.

WHAT REALLY HAPPENED TO AMUNDSEN AND SCOTT?

AMUNDSEN

Amundsen's uncharted route took him a total of 2,250 km, including a 3,000 metre climb up a steep, winding glacier. The five-man party scaled the glacier

Triumphant at the Pole – Amundsen poses before the Norwegian flag.

in four days, then shot all but 18 of the dogs, as the rest were not needed. They reached the South Pole on 14 December 1911.

After cooking a meal to celebrate, the Norwegians retraced their route, returning to Framheim on 26 January 1912.

SCOTT

Scott's motors soon broke down and the tractor-sledges had to be abandoned. Then the

The routes that Scott and Amundsen took across the frozen land of the South Pole.

ponies had to be shot. Less skilful in handling dogs, Scott sent their teams back when they reached the Beardmore Glacier. On 10 December they began to climb the glacier, dragging three sledges of supplies behind them. By 31 December Scott had decided to split his party, sending seven back and pressing on to the Pole with four others – Wilson, Oates, Bowers and Evans. They finally reached it on 18 January 1912 – only to find the Norwegian flag already flying there and a message from Amundsen.

THE RETURN

Scott's return march was a further series of disasters. The weather got much worse. Supplies of food and fuel ran low. Weaker and weaker, the men trudged slowly on. On

The final entry in Scott's diary shows that he knew there was no hope of rescue.

17 February Evans died after a severe fall. On 17 March Oates, suffering severely from frost-bitten feet, crawled out of the tent in a blizzard so that the rest could share out the food that was left. The last three struggled on for just 16 km further until another blizzard kept them in their tent for nine days. Scott knew they were close to a food-dump, but they could not reach it. The final entry in his diary is dated 29 March – "We shall stick it out to the end... but the end cannot be far."

The bodies of Scott, Wilson and Bowers were found by a search-party from Cape Evans on 12 November 1912.

AFTERWARDS

Amundsen became the first man to sail right round the Arctic Ocean and the first to fly across the Arctic in an airship. He disappeared on a flight over the Arctic two years later, searching for the airship of another explorer.

INDEX